People I've Known Loved & Hurt

Sahil Samji

BookLeaf Publishing
India | USA | UK

Presentation by *BookLeaf Publishing*

Web: www.bookleafpub.com

E-mail: info@bookleafpub.com

ISBN: 9789357697156

First edition 2023

DEDICATION

They say in school "listen to your teachers and focus on your studies, leave your friends alone, they'll only cause you trouble".

Funny enough I've been failed by teachers constantly, as have my loved ones. I have found rather, that my friends and loved ones alike have been and always will be my greatest teachers.

Go figure.

Simply put, I dedicate this book to the people I've known, the people I've loved, and the people I've hurt.

What a joy to not be alone in a world of such perceived solitude.

ACKNOWLEDGEMENT

A huge thank you to all my loved ones who have supported me through thick and thin, without you all I would be nothing short of a failure.

To my parents, whose unconditional love and support, however unorthodox, have been my foundation since I was conceived.

To my baby brother, who looks out for me with maturity, even if he's the younger one.

To Sheldon, who saw the strong resilient man in me before I even could.

To Joshua, whose light and life lessons guided me out of the darkness of my own mental torture, a teacher for the ages.

To Michael, who's supported me in Art and Poetry, through Hip-Hop, before I even knew I was capable of it, my brother in much more than arms.

To Caitlin, who, even thousands of miles away, is near and dear to my heart and built for us a home away from home where friendship can thrive.

To Rachelle, my non-congenital twin who can put a smile on my face and make me laugh till my ribs hurt, even on the brink of a mental breakdown.

And lastly, to Mariah, the woman who taught me how to love, and loved me for who I was, long before I knew the meaning of the word.

I love you all, with all my heart.

In memory of Willow, forever in my heart.

PREFACE

For most of my life, I entirely disregarded The Arts and saw little to no value in them. From childhood to very early adolescence scoffing at the idea of myself creating art or even being a creative person. I labeled myself with the complete inability to be "an artist". This may have been due to my somewhat sheltered upbringing or the shadow of doubt cast around the idea of Art and how it was thought of to be an utter waste of time and entirely unfruitful, at least in the culture I had been brought up in. Maturing from early adolescence, I found myself plagued with everything from addiction, homelessness, and surfing from institution to couch and right back around, a vicious cycle that left me a victim of my environment and surroundings for years. The turning point for me was when I discovered poetry. I took a creative writing course when I was haphazardly taking night classes in college, and after this, something in me sparked. It may have been something small, but in that period of time, I discovered something I had never considered before, an interest in the Arts. Along with it came a lifelong passion for writing and poetry which I carry with me to this day. It amazes me how such a small spark in such a dark time in my life completely changed the direction of my life for the better. For the better part of the time I've spent writing, I've focused on using writing as a tool of therapy as well as a form of self-expression and I realize that at its core it will always be such. Sometime along the way, I realized that however much I loved this method of expression, I developed a strong inability or rather unwillingness to write for or dedicate writing to anyone else. I realized the selfishness of such and while I still very much love writing for my own therapy, with this book I took on the challenge of creating pieces solely dedicated to the interactions I've had with others and deriving meaning from the strange, fascinating and wonderful people that I have encountered in my life.

An Ode to Mitch Welling

why do we come here?
where is my soul?
is it in my chest?
or somewhere out there
far far away?
my guess is we come to this earth
to dance and have fun
in the flames of a garden meant to burn

it doesn't bother me too much
i'm not scared to die
i know there's plenty to this life
and i'd be a coward to fear the crescendo
i'll pluck the chords till my fingers bleed
let my bones crash into holes of sound
and fall as soft as petals, as soft as ash
falling solar systems away

and maybe that's all it is
it's a shame we aren't soulmates
cause if i didn't know any better, i'd say this
feels pretty good

I'll carry this violet forever

i sat on the shore
as my eyes pierced the sun
it didn't burn
rather it glowed a soft purple
miles above the horizon
i watched it melt into the river
the soft purple spread into an indiscernible violet
it reflected shakily into the water from an
infinite sky

the emptiness made me shudder
i felt my heart pang, my muscles clenched
and the sobering realization that i am now alone
seeped in as the night softly spread across the
shore line
i griped with it for a moment
my bones went cold as the violet spread into my
pores, eating me alive
the fear of it all crashed into me
and every soft ripple of water felt like a
hurricane, shredding my insides out

suddenly something caught me
out of the corner of my eye
a pale white light
i turned my sight to the waning crescent
hanging softly in the sky

such a subtle light
burning brighter than any star
i pulled it out of the sky
and tucked it into a pocket
deep inside my heart
i knew right then and there
i'd never be alone again

20 minutes of Arbitrary Ambrosia

How sweet
How haphazardous
To run into you

Crashing into your skin felt something like a
supernova
A brilliant explosion of passion that left me
empty for weeks

How you sunk your teeth into my lips
The way we devoured each other as everyone
looked on
If they even existed at all
For a moment, all that existed was flesh
And carnal desire of

Parsing fragments of desire and drunken
memory
I can recall momentary pauses of satiation
As I laid my head on your chest

How my hands trembled, from eagerness or
perhaps fear, laid on your thigh, the memory of
your skin shaking them to the depth of physical
neurosis. Unconsciously bellowing the echoes of
longing straight to Heaven's door, rattling the
gates with seismic tremors.

The soft caress of your fingers running through
my hair, pulling strands of impurity out of my
skull, as delicately as Israfel plucked the strings
of Her Lyre and every deceitful lie of
self-deprecation I had built on the way to you
washed out of me, it was nothing short of
Divine.

The echoes thundered on
The melody danced along softly
The prism of mortality shook
As we weaved a hymn as graceful as snow
As graceful as nothing

It was a storm heaven would not soon forget
And yet the gates remained shut

And as I passed you
On my exit from the nightclub
I grabbed your arm
And left you with the most haphazardous kiss I
could conceive

And in that moment, I swear, I could hear angels
weep from above

I never got your name
(much less your number)

But I carry your memory, fondly as I can
A nameless supernova, etched into my heart

It feels wrong
I think I'll call you Honey
So sweet
So haphazardous

Cocoa Butter

How you dashed out of the night
And dug your ivory claws into my sheets
Your curiosity frightened me
Your high-strung pillars of morality
Stacked like child's play
In the sanctuary of my trauma
Salt in the wound
A gash that had been bleeding me dry
"You're gonna have to get over it"
The silence did little justice
To the anger swelling in my chest
The little boy in my head screamed
"How dare she ?! "
My every fiber wanted so badly to set aflame the
proverbial dollhouse you set me in

Crush it
Kick it
Stomp it

But as it did, as it always does, the gentle heart
shone through
It spoke to me of care, compassion, kindness,
forgiveness
And all those other pretty flowers in the garden
The Beautiful Garden of Introspection
In My Own Mind

The little boy rolled his eyes; petulantly as he
could
And ran off playfully, as little boys do

So I packaged your things
Your opinions of me
Your heart-shaped worldviews
Your daggers of curiosity
Your loosely scattered pillars of morality
And after a moment's reflection
In the palm of my hands, they appeared exactly
as they were
Child's play

So in these words, I'll wrap them as up as gently
as possible
And tuck them away, neatly
In the alcove of "things I'd rather forget"

And I'll kiss them goodbye
Just as I did you

Jezebel

flurry of pain
false decadence betrays you
Babylon would fall by your hand
should you not clench
to your victim complex
so tight
instead you're washed away
by pitiful men
who compensate their lack of morals
with deep pockets
i hear your cries
though they fall on deaf ears
i wish you resignation of your burdens
find your solace
find it far away from me

Petals

Petals

Your eyes cry for porcelain
It's so sad to see
Through tears of nectar
They can't see their own honey
Pools of sweetness
Their beauty lost to themselves
Quit letting porcelain boys
Pick apart your petals

Petals pt. 2: ?warmth≠comfort¿

her kisses are velvet
and yours are sweet
but i'd much prefer
the sting of something
i cannot have
over the taste of someone
who knows not what they hold
so i'll lament your sweetness
And let you go
return to my shed
buried under months of rubble
and chew away at sugarcane stems
strewn about
and through the bitterness of it all

maybe one day
i'll wish for warmth again

Daisy

Reckless teenage boy
Tried to mark my territory
Like a rabid dog, hungry without remorse
You held the balance of my heart in your hands
If any
I disfigured your beauty with my lips a flame
You had every reason to leave

That Pirate Heart of Yours (and why i didn't deserve it)

Oh how you dragged me out
From the bottom of the sea
Released me from my prison
My shackles cast from me

The time we spent was joyful
Every moment was bliss
Oh the grace to be atop your ship
For a castaway like me

And in your embrace I caught a sight,
of something so heavenly
And through your grace I found hope
but solace is what I sought

Your love burned bright
It nearly set me aflame
But it did little to light
This tortured heart in me

And so

I rose my flag, however false
The Flag of Mutiny

I had no ship but I took to the sea
to wretched waters for a wretch like me

though I cannot sail with you
and I won't have you drown with me
I am indebted to you
for all eternity

you freed me of my prison
you taught me how to swim
and for a tortured soul like me
that's all I'll ever need

An Ode to Oliver Sykes

How does one tackle solitude?
As a preferable state?
Or rather a painful one?
Can we consider our own company valuable in
relation to only itself?
Surely we must value ourselves profoundly
But pity, great pity to the solipsistic mind
For the beauty of self work, inner work
And the depth in which we value ourselves
Presents us with a great wealth
In which we can connect with others
In the depth of their own being

What a richness
To create a bond with another
Two souls alike
Held in hand at their very cores
What a joy to be known, from the heart
In the depths of our solitude
Not the slightest bit alone

So I raise a toast
To the people I've known
The people I've loved
And the people I've hurt
There is a hell, believe me, I've seen it

There is a heaven, let's keep it a secret

And the Willow Weeps

prison of flesh
you deserved better.
in death,
your memory crystallized
a statue of perfection
for you, in my mind

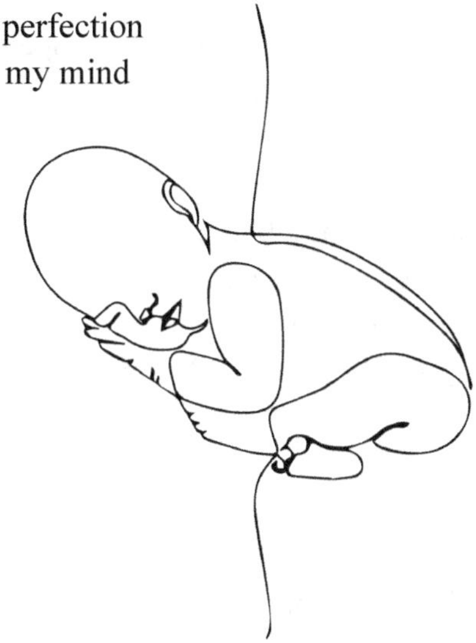

The Warm Winter Blanket of Falling Snow

Crash into my cavern
Tuck my skin into my room
Trade my desire for unfolding wishes
And a fervent faithful longing
Thoughtfulness worn thin
Love's currency, abundant and unspent
Its value cascades me soundly, however invisible
to most

Scorned by contradictions
Yet hollow to their glare
Set ablaze my place of worry
With botanics, green and beige

And as my fingers draw the shades
In this room I lay
I lay in respite
I lay down my spite
For its knife is edged on each side
And to stab or be stabbed, I resign

I trade my burning sun
For the ashes of winter
A paler ash of cold
Remnants of fire
In the ethereal ash of snow

And in this trap of metaphor
My love I hope you know
My sun is forever grateful
For your eternal blanket of snow

And I'm sure by now you know
I love you now
And I'll love you forever
My darling I love you so

The Twins

A recurring theme
How we came together
At the lowest point of my life
Darkness surrounding me
And you carried me through
Even kind enough to share your darkness with
me
A pale light
Putting cracks in my armor
And laying down my sword

To this day you're here
When I'm feeling lower then low
Cracking my ribs open
As I laugh till my face hurts
Gracious

Most run
But you never turned from my dark
And the pain I carry
Bubbling under the surface
Something so rare
A gem in the wasteland of time
The little sister I never had

And you know I'll be here for you
For now

For always & ever more

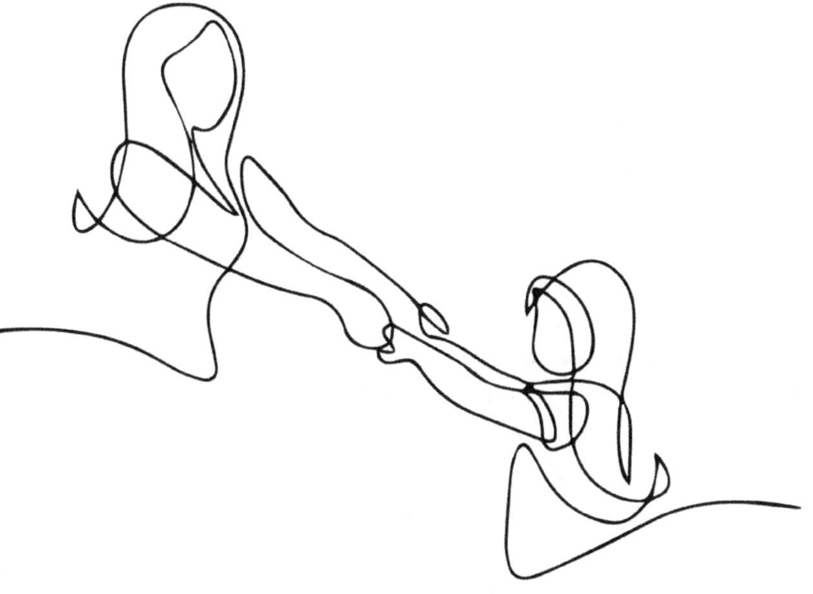

Game(r)s

I can't pinpoint where exactly we met
Or the very moment we've bonded
But I must admit you've been a shoulder to cry
on
Much more then I can count
And in this place
This sacred place
Friendship breathes so easily

For most of my life
The concept
Friendship
It was so foreign to me
As a child, through early adolescence
I never quite had friends like I do now
Flitting through time and space
Excluded from almost every group I'd
approached
An outcast in every sense of the word
But this space I feel welcome more then ever
It's almost effortless
Letting go of the worries of the day here

And we have you to thank
I've never liked establishments

And their administration
But you my dear friend
Are an administrator
I will love forever

So here's to the friendship that I never thought
possible
To the years spent laughing, crying
And sharing the most sublime moments
imaginable
To many more years to come
And to a home away from home

I am my brother's keeper

My relationship with men has always been
complicated
Tedious at best
To say I held a spite for them; an understatement
From betrayal
To ostracization
Insults on my integrity
And attacks on who I am
Race, stature and upbringing alike
Years of insecurity, boiling under the surface
Turned to turmoil
And a heavy bitterness
Like a black cloud hanging over me
But in the depths of this, brotherhood was
formed
To know you've both felt it too
To admit we've hurt and been hurt
Sharing the deepest, darkest secrets with each
other
With little to no reprehension
How beautiful
Battered from years of abuse
Standing taller than ever
The passage of time had not been kind to any of
us
We fought, laughed, argued and grew together

Becoming the exact modicum of what a man
should be
Brothers in more than blood
And if need be
blood as well
To the men I trust
I'd kill for you

Nothing quite lasts forever
But I'll be here,

Till my grave is dug
So just quiet down
And call when you're around

Parris, 5 years ago

I have a vague memory
Sitting in the subway terminal
Desolate as could be
Charging my phone, sat on the floor
Mud caking my jeans
I surely had no where to be
Going no where fast
And there you sat with me
As an equal
As a friend
Years of substance abuse had left me
A shell of a body
A rotten excuse for a man
But still we sat
Time and time again

You spoke to me of your dreams
Your character
Your ambitions
It was all so foreign to me
And the scoundrel in me pushed back
at every chance I got
That pitiful existence of mine tried, at times, to
vilify lessons impressed
And still you sat with me
As an equal
As a friend

Now I realise, that all along you had been
helping me unweave a tangled web of lies
wrapped around me for what I believed to be
comfort.
Now, as clear as day, I can see them for what
they were
Restraints

So the man I am today must thank you
Still today, we sit
As equals
As friends
But today I have dreams
Character
Ambition
Thank you for pulling out of The Mud

A song for Jessica, forever ago

A burst of laughter
That could pierce the hollowest of hearts
But mine was just that
Hollow
I'd hoped your beauty could fill my bones
Seeping into my casket
Instead it will nourish the earth
This gracious earth
That gave us a platform
To express the endearment
I had longed for my entire life
(until we collided)
And till the next time
Somewhere far, far away
My bubbling shooting star

**An Olive branch, high atop the tree, far
beyond the clouds**

Psychopathic predators
So-called leaders
Dressed in sheep skins
Legislating laws and toxifying medicine
Creating a vortex of poverty that swallows up
the land
But this isn't about them

Feverently dragging a cigarette, I asked you
"Do I seem insecure?"
"Yes" you replied
"But so am I"
The days were as slow as sludge
At the shit stain of Portage
A sorry excuse for rehabilitation
More like a den of baby wolves
Surviving off cream cheese crackers
And fits of "catcher in the rye"
I don't miss that horrid place

Though meeting you was desolate
Our time together was arguably worse
We spent our days, ingesting pounds of poison
for fun
Stole, begged and borrowed
Setting fire to common decency

It was a miserable existence
But in this we were brothers
And it was all we really knew

I still remember sitting on that couch
Matt was putting a needle in me, I was probably
too fucked up to stand
Much less mainline
I think I remember
You were picking through the carpet
Looking for a rock lost days ago
I cocked my head back on the couch, headed to
nirvana
I recall Matt yelling at you
"Cut that shit out man!"
As you continued to inhale possibly the most
grotesque pieces of lint known to man
Digging for a needle in a haystack, or rather a
diamond in the dumpster
And there I sat, a ghost on that couch
Blood rushing to my head
Something in me snapped
I grabbed my stuff and rushed hurriedly for the
door
You caught me

"You alright man?"

"I gotta go"

That was the beginning of the end
I don't think I've touched a spoon since
Not sure I've even seen you since
Save for the shitty business "opportunity" here
and there

Years later, on the metro home from work, I saw
Matt and we crossed eyes
He sat me down and told me the news
Try as I did, I could not hold back the tears
He hugged me with those massive bear arms of
his
A comfort on the worst of days, as long as you
were on his good side
He caught me up on his life
He seems to be doing well

These systems that chew us up and spit us out
Treat us like disposable scum
They had forsaken us
Left us for dead
We fought them, tooth and nail
But you never stopped fighting
Did you?

An Ode to Angel Olsen

i watch the leaves fall this season
as the sting of autumn rolls into the harsh burn
of a Canadian winter
i watch the burst of colours
how it disappears as vividly as it came
the emptiness that remains
is as apparent as it's being

much is to be learnt here
to self destruct is as natural as fall is to the
leaves, to decay is fate
neither is less poignant then the next
and the beauty of each is not in opposition but
rather in harmony with the other

as mesmerizing as it is
the explosion of colour happens not for the sake
of the eyes that watch
be like the leaves
Burn Your Fire For No Witnesses

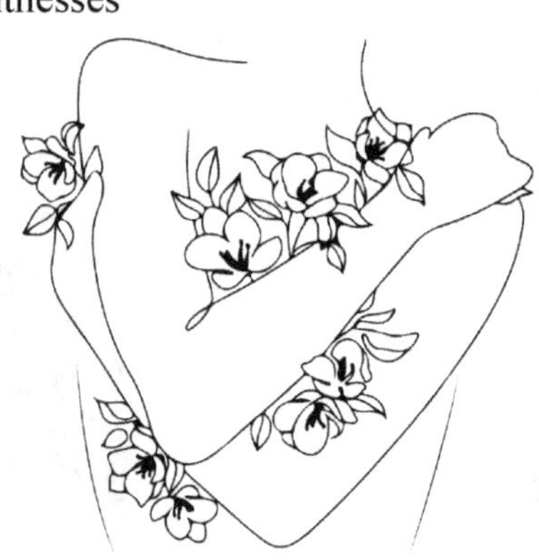

A letter to all my angels

please
realize your immense worth
and unparalleled value
don't let someone realize it for you
"you've got something special about you"
do not say
"really?"
"you think so?"
your answer should be
"i know"
they will try to syphon your light
they will use you as a catalyst
to amply their pitiful existence
do not let them
know your worth, rapture their deceit
meadow loves you

A bucket of Water

you poke holes in my bucket
surely for fun
but sometimes you stab
with an incessant gash
out pours the water i struggle to carry
that i strived to collect
i'm left cleaning floors
and mourning a week of work
and the love i've built
if even for only myself
is seeped away in a moment's neglect
I tell you it hurts
and You only laugh
and question why i wept

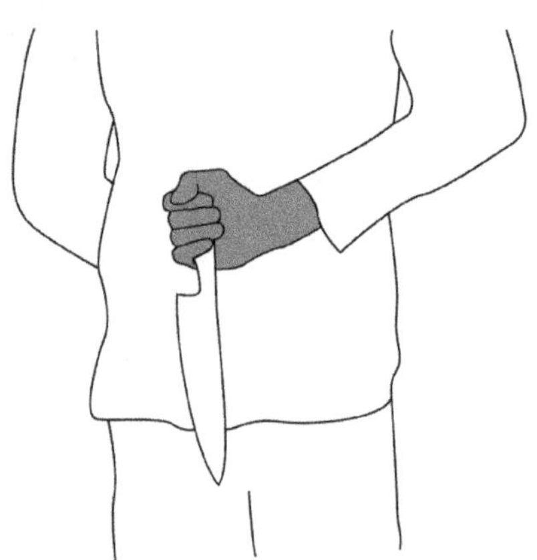

The Mirror

i wish i could step through the mirror and hug
that boy
instead of standing there and watching
An idle observer of My own sorrow
pathetic.

this barrier of overly blatant reflection that bars
me from my own consolations
such a cheap trick by an ever cheaper devil; the
illusion of solitude

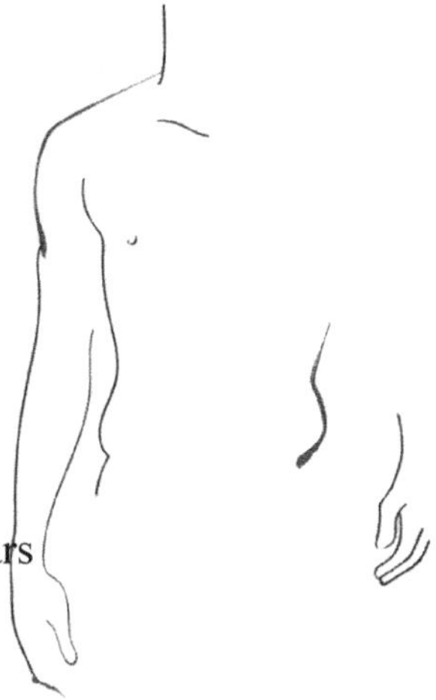

i know it's not fair
but i'm right here
my beautiful baby boy
and i promise you
you're not alone
i know it's not fair
but don't worry for too long
i'm right here to wipe your tears
you'll feel warmth again
i promise
give 'em hell

the judge
the jury
the execution

i'm thankful for my past self
who had to figuratively guillotine the people
who caused me intentional harm
and throw the ones, who did the same
unintentionally, into the dungeon of my mind
and space; awaiting parole.
and those who cause harmless trouble are given
a pass as i would hope the same courtesy
would be extended to me.
and to those i've caused harm in any way, i hope
you extend the same severity to me.
i aim to be just, whether merciful or severe.
may i be treated as i treat others